KINDLE PUBLISHING

Page intentionally left blank.

KINDLE PUBLISHING

A CLEAR GUIDE TO MAKING YOUR OWN BOOKS AND SELF-PUBLISHING ON AMAZON

SIMPLE STEPS TO MAKING MONEY ONLINE FOR BEGINNERS FROM START TO FINISH

1ST EDITION

By
James Bell
Copyright © 2017 by Hudson House Publishers
All rights reserved

Published by:
https://www.thinkselfpublishing.com

JOIN THE FREE VIDEO COURSE:

HOW TO MAKE 1K PER MONTH WITH KINDLE PUBLISHING

THINKSELFPUBLISHING.COM

HOW TO MAKE
1K PER MONTH WITH
KINDLE PUBLISHING

A Clear Plan with Simple
Steps for Beginners

Kindle Publishing 4

The hardest goal to achieve with self-publishing will be making the first 1K per month.

After reaching this goal increasing your monthly income becomes a simple mechanical process.

Learn the exact steps to reaching 1K by watching our FREE video course: **How to Make 1K Per Month with Kindle Publishing**.

To access the free course click the link below:

http://thinksp.net/1k

About the Author

I'm a full-time self-publisher, who enjoys the process of writing and starting businesses.

I've been self-publishing for around 3 years now and in that time I've managed to learn a little bit of what works, and what does not work, when it comes to self-publishing non-fiction books.

Before taking the plunge into self-publishing full-time I was a systems engineer by trade. My formal education was in computer science, and I still love technology.

— James Bell (Author)

TABLE OF CONTENTS

About the Author 6

Table of Contents 7

Send Questions, Send Feedback 15

Legal Notes 16

An Introduction to Self-Publishing and Making Money Online 17

How to Use This Book and What You Should Take-Away From It 21

How I Started Self-Publishing 22

How I View Myself and Self-Publishing 23

Getting Started with Kindle Publishing Properly: The 7 Steps to Live By 25

Your Day-to-Day Tasks When Getting Started with Kindle Publishing 26

Selecting a Niche to Publish In 27

Understanding the Niche and Its Role In the Success of an Internet Business 28

Self-Publishing: Past and Present 31

The Wide Self-Publishing Strategy of the Past and an Explanation of "Going Wide" 34

Why A Wide Publishing Style is Not Effective in Today's Marketplace 36

"Going Wide" Summarized: Things to Remember 37

The Reality of Implementing a Wide Publishing Style Today...................... 38

The Narrow Style of Publishing i.e. the Most Effective Way to Self-Publish .. 40

The Benefits of a Narrow Publishing Style and Its Relation to Building a Brand 42

The Hostility of Readers in Certain Niches Toward Self-Published Authors 44

More Benefits to Publishing Narrow: The Favorability of Readers Toward Your Brand 46

Selecting A Niche Important Things to Remember 47

Why Building a Brand Matters 49

Selecting a Niche: Rules of Thumb .. 50

- Be an Expert, Be Passionate, or at a Bare Minimum Be Interested........... 52
- An Implementation of a Narrow Publishing Strategy........................... 54
- Quality Control and Its Importance In the Long-Term Viability of Your Self-Publishing Business.......................... 56
- What It Means to Provide Value and the Simplest Method for Delivering It 57
- Quality Control, Providing Value, and Their Relation to the Outline of a Book 60
- Outlining in Self-Publishing 62
- 3 Parts to a Great Outline 63
- Finding a Book's Most Important Topics 64
- Adding Questions to Your Book's Outline 67
- Techniques for Using the Outline's Questions When Writing a Book...... 68
- Adding Outside Resources to a Book's Outline 71

Methods of Getting Your Book Written and the Best Method to Choose 73

Honest Reasons Why You Should NOT Write Your Own Books 73

A Straightforward Method for Writing a Book and How to Use an Outline .. 75

The Simplest Technique for Performing Research 78

How Large Should a Self-Published Book Be? 80

Mechanisms for Working Productively 84

Forcing Focus with the Pomodoro Technique 86

The Role of Enthusiasm in Work and Self-Publishing................................. 89

Outsourcing for the Best Chance at Success... 90

The 2nd Aspect of Self-Publishing A Book: The Book Cover...................... 92

A Normal Workflow for Designing a Book Cover When First Getting Started 94

Platforms for Outsourcing and the Best Uses for Each 96

Hire a Designer Who Will Provide Their Work in Multiple Formats 98

Using Stock Photography and a Warning Against Using Free Stuff ... 99

Simplified Principles for Book Cover Design 101

The Difficulty of Building a Team .. 102

How to Find Your Writer and the Specifics of Job Postings 104

The Interviewing Process and Hiring 105

Paying Hourly vs. Using Fixed Price Milestones 107

A Simplified Workflow for Paying a Freelancer 108

Managing a Team of Freelancers Effectively and a Simple Technique for Forcing Productivity 111

Know What You Want and Communicate It Clearly 113

A Management Style to Avoid When Hiring Freelancers 114

Becoming an Ideal Client That Freelancers Will Enjoy Working With 116

Procedures for Avoiding Dishonest Freelancers and Preventing Plagiarism 118

Effectively Using the Cloud While Self-Publishing 120

Setting Up Google Drive for Maximum Productivity and the Importance of Cloud Collaboration 121

Use Google Drive. Dropbox Will Waste Your Time 124

Putting It All Together: Where You Are In the Self-Publishing Process 124

Ensuring All Your Book's Content is Unique i.e. Checking for Plagiarism 126

Effective Proofreading: A 2-Step Process 128

Your Main Goal When Editing an Outsourced Book 130

Kindle Direct Publishing vs. Createspace: The Main Self-Publishing Platforms 132

Why You Must Submit Your Content to Both Platforms 133

Specifics of Formatting a Book for Digital Publication 134

Addressing the Front and Back Matter of Your Books 136

Supplementary Pages to Include in the Front Matter of Your Books 136

Supplementary Pages to Include in the Back Matter of Every Book You Publish 139

Conventional Book Formatting Practices 142

Conventional Line Spacing Practices and the Application of Section Headers 144

Important Aspects Related to Formatting a Book for Print Publication 147

The Final Step in Publishing i.e. Submitting Content to the Different Platforms 149

Understanding the Two Parts to a Good Book Blurb or Production Description 150

Two Methods for Getting a Book Blurb or Product Description Created Efficiently.. 153

Your First Book is Officially Published. Now What? 155

Staying True to the Subtitle: Ensuring the Simplicity of Getting Started.... 156

30 Simple Steps to Getting Started 158

SEND QUESTIONS, SEND FEEDBACK

Feel free to send any feedback or questions directly to me. I will try my best to answer everyone
james@thinkselfpublishing.com.

— James Bell (Author)

LEGAL NOTES

ALL RIGHTS RESERVED. NO PART OF THIS BOOK MAY BE REPRODUCED OR TRANSMITTED IN ANY FORM OR BY ANY MEANS. PHOTOCOPYING, POSTING ONLINE, AND / OR DIGITAL COPYING IS STRICTLY PROHIBITED UNLESS WRITTEN PERMISSION IS GRANTED BY THE BOOK'S PUBLISHING COMPANY. LIMITED USE OF THE BOOK'S TEXT IS PERMITTED FOR USE IN REVIEWS WRITTEN FOR THE PUBLIC.

An Introduction to Self-Publishing and Making Money Online

In today's connected world of social media and online shopping. It seems that more and more people are interested in making money online. And if you are reading this book then, you most likely, are one of these people.

One thing to realize when it comes to making money online is: there are legitimately a thousand different ways to do it. And when we say a thousand, we mean that.

You can make money re-selling books on eBay, email marketing, blogging, podcasting, YouTubing, private labeling, drop-shipping, and so on. Even within Kindle publishing there are different ways to make money with it.

But, regardless of the method you choose within Kindle publishing, or if you choose to make money in a completely different type of internet business. You have to stick with it. Do not jump from one thing to the next.

The best method for being successful in any internet business is to pick something and stick with it for at least 6 months and really focus on doing the same thing. Even though 6 months is not a long time to be doing something, forcing yourself to stick with one thing for 6 months should help you to see some type of results from your work.

And this should be your overall goal when getting started with kindle publishing.

After 6 months of staying consistent. You want to see results from your efforts. If you stick with self-publishing, the results you should see after 6 months, is a consistent amount of monthly royalties. The specific amount of royalties will depend largely on the number of books you have published and the quality of your works.

There are three main types of books you can self-publish:

- Non-fiction

- Fiction e.g. romance / sci-fi
- Public domain

This book will teach you how to make money self-publishing non-fiction books. If you desire to publish other than non-fiction then you should do either one of 2 things:

1. Jump right in and get started by hiring a freelancer to write your book, or begin writing it yourself.
2. Hire a mentor, buy a course, or read a related book that will help you get started.

You must avoid not taking action because the longer you wait the easier it will be for you to continue procrastinating. And the more you procrastinate the more the market for self-publishing may change and the harder it will be for you to mentally get started.

Taking action quickly after you have come to a clear decision on something you want to do, is the best course of action for achieving a goal. Kindle publishing is no different.

If you've been thinking about self-publishing for a while, and you are reading this book, then finish reading this book in a few hours and take action!

Before you get started make sure that you have a quiet place to work without constant disruptions, and make sure you have a reliable computer with an active internet connection. Once you have these things, and a bank account, make sure you are serious about self-publishing, and make sure you are ready to mentally commit for at least 6 months to get started.

This book is a straight forward guide to the most important aspects of self-publishing non-fiction books on Amazon. There is very minimal fluff, there are no diagrams, or images. The book is divided into sections.

How to Use This Book and What You Should Take-Away From It

To get the most from this book. Start from the beginning and read the entire book in one sitting. It should probably take you about 3 to 4 hours to complete at a slow reading pace, for faster readers it will take less.

The goal of this book is to convey the most important things you need to know to get started with self-publishing. The goal of this book is not to teach you every single detail of the self-publishing process because it is not necessary to know every detail when you get started.

When getting started, you need to understand the basics so you can take proper action immediately, and get started the right way. Once you have begun you will learn as you go. And as you continue to work, you can ask relevant questions based on your problems or experiences. This is the best method for success.

How I Started Self-Publishing

When I started self-publishing years ago, my mentor gave me only a portion of the information that will be conveyed in this book. The rest I figured out while actually publishing books over the years.

When I learned about Kindle publishing, and learned the websites to use. I jumped in and immediately began over-paying for everything. Freelancers gave me copy and pasted work, and I didn't know until it was published. I paid more for a book cover, then the actual writing in the book. And I made numerous other mistakes. But by getting started, and getting books published, something happened. I was making sales, even with all the mistakes.

The sales proved to me that self-publishing would work, and that the information my mentor shared was valuable when applied. I kept going and kept learning over time.

It is very important that you do the same as well. Get started and stick with it. Consistency will pay off over time. And once you begin and actually make a few sales, those sales, should spur you on and prove that self-publishing is not a waste of your time or money.

So let's jump into the meat and potatoes of the book and learn the most important aspects to getting started.

How I View Myself and Self-Publishing

I view myself as an entrepreneur not as an author. I like writing, because journaling has always been a personal hobby, but I like building profitable businesses more.

This book is written for people who want to start a business, it is not intended for aspiring authors who desire to be known for their writings.

If you are reading this book as an aspiring author you may find some benefit, because the book will explain a method for profiting from your work without needing conventional industry approval. But the book was not written with aspiring authors in mind.

This book was written for serious people who desire to build a profitable and sustainable business and self-publishing offers a platform for doing this.

Getting Started with Kindle Publishing Properly: The 7 Steps to Live By

There are 7 main steps to publishing a book:

1. Selecting a niche to publish in and selecting subsequent topics for your books.
2. Identifying the most important information that your book should contain and creating a comprehensive outline for each book you will publish.
3. Getting your book written.
4. Getting a book cover designed and created.
5. Ensuring that your book's content is unique i.e. checking for plagiarism.
6. Formatting the book for print and digital publication.
7. Publishing the book.

Once the 7th step has been successfully completed you should continually repeat the process and try to make improvements.

Your Day-to-Day Tasks When Getting Started with Kindle Publishing

Your day to day work when getting started with self-publishing will be to systematically go through these steps. After completing the first 7 steps you will have a book available for sale. Once the book is published you want to repeat the 7 steps and work on doing it faster. The process of repeating and improving is the 8th step and it is a very important step.

Making more income from royalties with self-publishing is publishing more books. This is why consistency is extremely important in those first 6 months of getting started.

Selecting a Niche to Publish In

The first step to self-publishing a non-fiction book on amazon is to choose a niche. Picking an appropriate niche is essential to success and the way you select a niche will relate to your overall publishing strategy.

When you are first getting started with self-publishing you have to pick an overall strategy that you will follow during the months to come as you build your business.

There are two styles to publishing non-fiction books on amazon. The first style of publishing is implementing a wide strategy, and the 2nd style is implementing a narrow publishing strategy.

Before we delve into the details of wide vs. narrow, and which style of publishing is the best. We must discuss what a niche is. This may seem like an obvious topic for any person with some knowledge about self-publishing or any person with some knowledge of making money online. But if you are completely new to the idea of self-publishing or making money online then you might not understand exactly what a niche is.

UNDERSTANDING THE NICHE AND ITS ROLE IN THE SUCCESS OF AN INTERNET BUSINESS

To avoid giving long and boring definitions a niche is a "particular segment of a market".

In other words, a niche is a unique thing that matters only to a certain group of people. It's very important that you understand this. A niche is something that only a certain group of people care about.

Anything can be a niche given that only a certain segment of the general population cares deeply about that thing.

For example any hobby is a niche.

Golfing is a niche because only a certain group of people care deeply about golfing. And golf is a specific segment of the sports market.

Intermittent fasting is a niche because it represents a segment of the diet / health and fitness market.

Gardening is a niche because it represents a certain segment of the general population that likes to plant things and watch the things they plant grow.

Hopefully you are getting the point.

A niche is a unique thing that only a particular group of people care about. Niches have become more and more important as the internet has grown in popularity. Because the internet has created an environment where people spend their time only browsing things they personally care about. And those things that people are spending their time browsing are niches.

Any successful online business will focus solely on making money in specific niches. And likewise, to be successful with self-publishing niches will be very important. Based on the publishing strategy you choose the way you select a niche will be different.

Self-Publishing: Past and Present

People have been self-publishing for about 10 to 15 years now as we know it today. As a result of this, the strategies that worked 7 to 10 years ago are not the best strategies to deploy in the current marketplace.

We mentioned earlier that there are two strategies to self-publishing. A wide strategy, and a narrow strategy. One of these strategies was very popular 7 to 10 years ago and this strategy is also the main strategy that newcomers will implement when first getting started. It is the publishing style of "going wide".

The reason an old strategy like going wide can still exist to this day is due to the fact that as time continues more and more people are learning about self-publishing. And these people are following the conventional advice given by online coaches. Most online coaches will teach people to "go wide".

You may be wondering to yourself what is going wide? And of course we are going to explain exactly what it means. But before we go into learning what "going wide" means. Remember that this style of publishing was very effective in the past, and to this day most newcomers will get started in this manner.

Publishing in this manner, will actually work, if you stick with it. But it is important to note. That this style of publishing is NOT the recommended strategy of this book, nor is it the best way to self-publish if you are getting started today.

We will discuss wide publishing only because you should understand how people will be competing with you, and because it can still make you money.

But remember even though "going wide" can work. It is not the BEST way to self-publish nowadays. Later on in the book we will learn the recommended strategy. But for now let's discuss how people have been publishing in the past, and how newcomers will be competing with you.

The Wide Self-Publishing Strategy of the Past and an Explanation of "Going Wide"

"Going wide" is a self-publishing strategy that says you should publish books on any topic given that the topic of the book is a popular one. The idea is: you as the publisher would define a certain set of criteria for a book topic. You would then go and find books that meet your criteria. Once you have found a number of books that meet this criteria you would then publish your own personal replicas of these books.

7 to 10 years ago, when the publishing marketplace was not as crowded, this type of strategy was extremely effective. It worked well because, for every book topic which was popular on amazon, there were only a few other books discussing the same information.

So as the person desiring to self-publish new books you would come into the marketplace and approach the same topic from a different angle. You would try to provide a new point of view, and deliver new information which was missing from the books already published on the same topic.

Consumers looking to casually buy things naturally want choices when purchasing. Typically a person enjoys browsing multiple books on related topics before finally making the decision to buy.

So back in the day when the marketplace was less crowded. There was a real opportunity to re-publish popular book topics and actually provide more value to readers by creating more content for them to choose from.

Why A Wide Publishing Style is Not Effective in Today's Marketplace

The problem with a wide style of publishing is: it worked years ago, and the marketplace is different from the old one. The current marketplace is crowded and has significant choice.

For example if you go on amazon right now, and do a search for any random non-fiction topic. You will find that for every topic you search there are multiple books on the same topic. If you attempted to re-publish the same information and try to add more value for readers. It would be a very hard task because readers already have significant choice.

If your goal was to re-publish the same information but focus on writing about the things that are missing from the other books on the same topic. You would have a hard time doing this as well because with so many books covering the same topic there isn't much you can add which has not already been addressed in other books.

"Going Wide" Summarized: Things to Remember

At this point understand for the past 10 years most self-publishers who published non-fiction books, had a wide publishing style. Meaning the publisher was creating books on any topic as long as the topic was popular. The goal was to replicate popular works already published and provide more value to readers by addressing what was missing from other books discussing the same topic.

Also understand that years ago this was an effective strategy because readers did not have as much choice when looking for things to purchase, and there was room for improving most books.

The Reality of Implementing a Wide Publishing Style Today

Also remember that if you started self-publishing today, in the current marketplace, and you implemented this strategy i.e. you sought to only publish books on very popular topics. Despite this not being the best method to choose. It will still make you money. The reason this style still works is there are so many people looking for things to buy on amazon that a new publisher can make money re-publishing other books, and provide more things for readers to buy.

For the most part, most online coaches will still say this is an effective strategy. And most new comers to self-publishing will still implement this style. And the fact that most people will still publish in this manner is a good thing for you.

It's good because you are reading this book and since you are reading this book you will learn to implement a different style of self-publishing that is more effective over the long term and completely different.

By reading this book and implementing the style of publishing it teaches. You will have less people competing with you directly. Because most people will be publishing wide, and competing amongst themselves.

A wide publishing strategy can make you money, but it is not the best publishing strategy. We have already discussed how long people have been self-publishing. And we have also discussed that most people over this time have been using the same strategy. Even further, most newcomers to the business of self-publishing will implement the same strategy of the past.

Everyone doing the same thing, and publishing in the same manner, has created a fairly crowded marketplace with a lot of the same content. It has also created an opportunity for people to self-publish in a new style. The opportunity for newcomers is to publish with a "narrow style".

THE NARROW STYLE OF PUBLISHING I.E. THE MOST EFFECTIVE WAY TO SELF-PUBLISH

A "narrow publishing strategy" is the best strategy for competing in today's publishing marketplace. The narrow style of publishing is the method I use in my self-publishing business, and it is the self-publishing method you should use, when getting started. The narrow style of self-publishing is also, the recommended strategy of this book.

With a narrow publishing style rather than publishing books on any topic. You are instead going to focus on publishing within only 1 niche. This means ALL your books will be published regarding one general subject or category. And each individual book that you publish will deal with one specific aspect of the niche.

This subsequently means that when you implement a narrow publishing style. All your books will be related. This is strikingly different from the wide publishing strategy of lore. With a wide strategy, if you published 100 books, you would have 100 books covering 100 different unrelated topics. With a narrow style, if you published 100 books you would have 100 books, all related to one niche, and therefore 100 books covering 100 different aspects of that one particular niche.

A narrow publishing strategy works because by focusing on one niche, and dealing with all aspects of that niche you position yourself and your brand as an authority within the niche.

By positioning yourself as an authority within the niche you subsequently prove to readers you are an expert on the topic. After spending months publishing in this manner and by also publishing a significant number of books within your given niche people will, over time, begin to associate you and your brand with the given niche.

The Benefits of a Narrow Publishing Style and Its Relation to Building a Brand

Obviously a narrow publishing style has benefits. The main benefit of which is it builds a brand which will become a recognizable name in the marketplace. It must also be mentioned that getting traction with this style of publishing takes time. This is why you have to stick with self-publishing and not give up after 2 months.

Building a brand will take a significant amount of time. Because it will take a significant amount of time to build a library of works all revolving around a particular niche.

But once you have built this brand you will find that the long-term viability of your self-publishing business increases. As time goes on and your books are available for sale the longevity will add to your position as an authority in the marketplace.

The shear fact that your brand name or pen name has multiple books on the same topic, and has had books published for a certain amount of time, will help over the long term. Having books with a sales history will give readers a more positive attitude toward your works. And it will again establish you as an expert within the niche.

A sad truth that must be recognized is the overall quality of many self-published books is decreasing. This is due to people jumping into the market with a wide strategy, focusing solely on making money in the short-term. You will rarely find authors who focus on becoming authorities in their niche and publishing a large volume of works all regarding one particular subject.

The Hostility of Readers in Certain Niches Toward Self-Published Authors

People are publishing wide and creating 100s of unrelated books, and not controlling the quality of their works. Most pen names and brands are not seen as authority figures, because self-publishers are not trying to be authorities and sadly this trend will continue. The fact that the marketplace is becoming more and more crowded and people are not controlling their quality is causing some hostility amongst readers toward self-published authors.

Certain niches have more hostile readers than others, and this is because certain niches have become magnets for self-publishers with a wide publishing method. These niches see 100s of books republished on the same topic, with no depth to the works, and no depth to the publishing brand or pen name.

Of course this situation is not ideal for readers, because, at the moment, they do not need more choice when purchasing, readers need more depth. Although the state of self-publishing non-fiction books may not be getting better for readers, because publishers do not care about longevity, or building an authoritative brand. This non-ideal state helps you as the self-publisher just getting started.

Given that you are reading this book, you can focus on building a brand and positioning yourself as an authority within your niche by implementing our recommend style of publishing narrow.

More Benefits to Publishing Narrow: The Favorability of Readers Toward Your Brand

Another benefit to publishing with a narrow style and only focusing on providing the best quality books on one topic within a particular niche is: readers will be much more favorable to your works because you've positioned yourself as an authority in the niche.

By publishing multiple works specific to one niche, we have already established that this will position you as an authority. When readers see that you have multiple books covering only one topic they are less likely to think of you as someone just trying to make money with books.

This increased favorability will hold true even if you are publishing books that are not too large in size. The fact that your brand will have multiple books within one niche will make up for many things that readers will otherwise see as unfavorable. But in order to realize this increased favorability you have to focus on dealing with only one niche, and you must avoid jumping around to different subjects. Do not start multiple pen names, only start one, and build it.

Selecting A Niche Important Things to Remember

So the important things to take away from the first step to self-publishing are niche selection is very important.

You can choose one of two publishing styles if are publishing non-fiction books. You can either implement a wide publishing strategy or a narrow one. A wide publishing strategy will put you with all the other self-publishers who have been publishing books over the past 10 years and you will be competing with newcomers who enter the market using the conventional wisdom of online coaches. But if implemented consistently a wide publishing style can still make you money, because there is a large demand for content on amazon, but implementing a wide strategy is not the best strategy.

Remember that the second method of self-publishing is using a narrow style and this is the recommended method publishing if you want the best chance for sustainable long term income.

Implementing a narrow publishing style means selecting only one main niche. This niche can be dieting, gardening, golfing, or anything you care or know about. Once you have selected this niche you will publish books only within this one given topic. Each book you publish should cover a different aspect of the chosen main niche.

Continuing this strategy over time will position you as an authority within your chosen niche and create a brand that is synonymous with the given niche.

Once you have built a recognizable brand, and this will come over time as you publish more books, readers will have a more positive image of your works and be less hostile toward your books and more likely buy more of your other works.

WHY BUILDING A BRAND MATTERS

Building a real brand will shield you from the negative effects of the crowded self-publishing marketplace. And building a brand will keep you unaffected by newcomers entering the market with a wide style.

After you have built a brand, and stuck with publishing in one niche for a given amount of time, like let's say 6 months, and you have published multiple books all regarding the same niche. You will find yourself shielded from people trying to compete with you directly because it will take a lot of work for someone to come and replicate everything you have done. It is very possible to do, and someone may try to do it. But the fact that you will have built the brand first, you'll have the benefit of sales history.

Being the first to build a brand within a niche and having your books available for sale over a longer period of time will give you more organic traffic from Amazon, and your books will rank higher than related works published after you.

Therefore do not worry about people copying you. Focus on being the first to tackle a niche and become an authority within it.

SELECTING A NICHE: RULES OF THUMB

General rules to follow when selecting a main niche for your narrow publishing strategy is to pick something you are an expert in. This is the first course of action when selecting a niche to target. If you are not an expert in any given subject then pick something you are passionate about, something you care about deeply. If all else fails and you are not an expert in anything or there is nothing you care deeply about. Then select a niche you are generally interested in, or something you would like to learn more about.

A narrow publishing strategy will force you to deal with a given niche and subject for a long time because all your book topics will be coming from within that one niche. It is best to choose something you know, because if you understand the niche, it will be easier for you to select more topics within the niche to publish books on.

Being an expert in a particular niche, or having a good amount of experience with a niche, will help to add personality to your books.

Be an Expert, Be Passionate, or at a Bare Minimum Be Interested

Being an expert does not mean you must be a doctor, or a software engineer. These things are great, but being an expert can also mean being a mom, or a parent, or being a gardener, or a cook. Anything you have significant experience with qualifies you as an expert in this case. And most people have some expertise in something. Try to spend some time brainstorming before selecting a niche to publish in.

If you are not an expert in any given thing you should select a main niche that is related to something you care about.

Being passionate about a topic will give you enthusiasm and make it easier to continue publishing about the same thing for an extended period of time. Being passionate about a topic or understanding it personally will shield you from getting bored.

Getting bored with a niche will most likely cause you to publish books in a new niche, or possibly quit publishing all together and we want to avoid these outcomes at all cost.

When selecting a niche, if there is nothing you care about, or have experience with, then select a topic you are interested in learning. By publishing books within that given niche you will be learning more about that topic. And given that you are interested in this thing, it should be easier for you continue publishing and stick with it.

For example let's say you are not an expert in anything. Let's also say you are not passionate about anything. But let's assume that maybe you are trying to lose weight and get healthy. In this case you should choose health and wellness as your niche and publish books about diets. Your general interest in losing weight and improving your lifestyle should make writing books on weight loss beneficial and somewhat enjoyable.

An Implementation of a Narrow Publishing Strategy

Before leaving the topic of niche selection. Here is an example of how a narrow publishing strategy would be implemented. Remember that with a narrow style you will focus on building a brand and positioning yourself as an authority within a niche. Therefore, one broad niche will be selected, and subsequently all your book topics will be drawn from within the niche. Everything you publish will be related and you will spend at least 6 months dealing with the same thing.

Let's continue with the assumptions made in the last section i.e. you are not an expert on anything, nor are you truly passionate about anything in particular. But you intend on getting healthy and improving the quality of your life. In this case your niche would be health and wellness, with a focus on weight loss.

Weight loss will be your overall niche and the topics for your books should fall under the weight loss category. For this example, if your niche is weight loss your book topics should be different diets.

Implementing a narrow publishing style with health and wellness as your niche would require you to spend some time researching different types of diets, and listing out as many as you can. Each diet that you find will be its own book. So maybe you will have a book on the Ketogenic Diet, another on Intermittent Fasting, another book on the Mediterranean Diet, another on Veganism, etc.

Once you have created a long list of diets and identified as many as possible. You would then move to the next step in the publishing process which is creating outlines for the individual books.

Quality Control and Its Importance In the Long-Term Viability of Your Self-Publishing Business

If you want to make money with self-publishing over the long term then you need to focus on quality control. You must publish good books, with good quality. This means avoiding grammar mistakes and avoiding errors in formatting your works.

This is very important.

If you can maintain consistency in your publishing efforts and continue to publish books at a steady rate and control the quality of your books. You will most likely see your income grow overtime and you will hopefully find success if you stick with publishing for long enough and grow your library of works.

It cannot be stressed enough how important quality control is. In the beginning it will be easy to keep your quality high and consistent, and you will definitely care about the quality of the works you are publishing. But overtime as your publishing efforts grow and you begin to create more books quality control becomes harder at scale.

WHAT IT MEANS TO PROVIDE VALUE AND THE SIMPLEST METHOD FOR DELIVERING IT

Along with controlling quality the information you publish must be good as well. To create good content you must focus on providing value to your readers. And the best method to provide the most value to your readers is to focus on dealing with every topic you publish fully. For every book you publish you most focus on writing about the most important aspects of that subject.

When a person reads your book, they should not feel like something was missing after the book is completely read. If you spend some time browsing self-published non-fiction books and look at 3 or 2 star reviews. Many of the reviews will cite that the book was missing something that the reader determined to be important. Sometimes these types of reviews are unavoidable because a reader will have unrealistic expectations for the book they are purchasing. But oftentimes these bad reviews can be avoided if you make providing value a priority in your publishing and put significant effort into determining what is important regarding a certain subject.

Identifying the most important aspects of a subject is done through research. As you perform the research needed to create an outline you will find and list the most important things for readers to learn and these subjects will be discussed in your books.

Regardless of the length of the books you choose to publish. Your main focus when publishing should be to control quality and provide value. And to provide the most value you must address the most important aspects of every topic you write about.

If the quality of your books is good and you do not miss anything important, you will satisfy most readers. And satisfied readers will be likely purchase other books from you given you have something they are interested in.

Quality control and value delivery are your two main focuses after selecting a niche to publish in.

QUALITY CONTROL, PROVIDING VALUE, AND THEIR RELATION TO THE OUTLINE OF A BOOK

We have been talking about the importance of quality control in self-publishing, and how providing value should be your utmost priority. We also identified that providing value is, controlling the quality of your books and making sure your books cover all the important topics related to its subject matter.

The way you link these things together is with the outline. The outline is the key to ensuring that a book is full and dense. A good outline produces a good book, in in most cases. And outlining is the 2nd step in the publishing process. Before getting into the specifics of outlines and how to properly make one. Remember that an outline can NEVER be too detailed or too long. And the point of your outline is to not only identify the most important topics for a particular book, the outline should also dictate the flow of information throughout the book. A proper outline is organized. Meaning that you are conscience of when readers are being introduced to certain topics.

Outlining in Self-Publishing

If you do a search for books on Kindle publishing it will be hard to find one that stresses the importance of an outline. But if you want long term success in self-publishing and you want the best chance for reaching your goals with self-publishing you have to pay significant attention to this step in the publishing process.

Throughout the entire 7 step process of publishing you should give the same amount of attention to each step. Do not neglect any steps. Neglect will show over time as you continue to publish more books.

Especially, do not neglect the outlining stage. Of all the steps in the publishing process outlining will most likely be the one that you start to neglect overtime. Try to avoid this, and make sure you allocate a good number of hours to sitting and focusing on getting a proper outline completed before you publish a book. Do not rush this step.

3 Parts to a Great Outline

An outline should be one word document containing three types of information:

1. Outside resources
2. A list of the most important subjects regarding the book's topic
3. Questions

Most of your outline should be a bulleted or ordered list. This list should contain the most important subjects of the book that is being written.

The longer and more detailed your outline is the better a book it will produce. This fact holds true regardless how long the book you are publishing is. A longer more detailed outline will produce a more valuable book to your readers.

This idea of creating an outline seems so simple, but it is very powerful and you should not neglect it. When publishing a book make sure to spend at least 2 hours creating an outline before moving on to the next step. And 2 hours is minimum, for a larger book you should to spend more time making the outline. Increasing the size of an outline is the easiest way to increase the size of a book.

FINDING A BOOK'S MOST IMPORTANT TOPICS

The bread and butter of your outline is the bulleted listing of the book's most important topics. Creating this bulleted list is where most of your time should be spent.

To identify the main topics of a book and the most important things to write about consult other books on the same subject. Finding other books on the same topic is easy because you can look at your competition online. Search the marketplace and online book retailers for books related to your topic.

The subject you are writing about will determine the number of related books you will be able to find. The more books you can find, the better. Once you have identified books that are related. You want to browse the table of contents of each book and make notes regarding the things being mentioned and focused on throughout the books.

As you are researching and looking at the table of contents of other books you should be creating your personal outline, taking notes of the different things you are finding. The more books you search the better because you will find more topics for your outline's main bulleted list.

Try to spend a majority of the time you allocate for outlining to browsing other books and noting the information you find in their table of contents. This information will be crux of your outline and also the bulk of your book.

Other self-published books are a good resource for making notes, but you should prefer authoritative texts on your subject. Textbooks and manuals are the best source because these books will have very detailed table of contents.

If the book you are publishing has little to no related books then you will have to look online to make your notes. Use general searches and forums to draw information.

When creating your bulleted list of important topics to cover be conscience of the flow of information. This means before you add a given topic to the outline you should ask yourself where the information best is placed.

Ask yourself, when is the best time for a reader to be introduced to the given topic? For example, should the topic be placed in the beginning of the book? The middle of book? The end of the book? Should the topic be introduced after another topic is introduced or vice versa?

Adding Questions to Your Book's Outline

After you have done a sufficient amount of research and built a detailed listing of the most important topics for your book you want to move on the 2nd most important aspect of your outline which is questions.

Depending on your topic you should begin to ask yourself questions regarding the subject. Anything you would like to know as a reader should be written down into the outline. List as many question as possible because it should be fairly easy for you come up with questions regarding a given subject.

Adding questions should be the 2nd task you complete when creating an outline but since you will be reading this section before you make your first outline. You can jot down any questions that come to mind as you are performing your main research to make the bulleted list.

The questions you list in your outline can be used in multiple ways when the book is written.

Outlines are made to aid the writer. Outlines lists all the information that should be researched before the book is written. As such, the questions in the outline can be used in two different ways by the writer of the book.

TECHNIQUES FOR USING THE OUTLINE'S QUESTIONS WHEN WRITING A BOOK

The first way in which a writer can the use the outline's questions is to begin performing their main research. Going topic by topic through the bulleted list of important things to cover. As each topic is selected the writer would save and read resources to come to an understanding of the thing they are researching. Once the writer has completed their research they would answer all the questions listed in the outline then begin the process of writing. If a question cannot be answered the writer would then perform more research to answer the question then continue writing.

The second way the questions can be used in the writing process is, the questions can be answered before the main research is begun.

Answering the questions will serve as preliminary research for the writer. Then once all the questions have been answered adequately the writer would then begin to perform the main research on the bulleted points. Once all the research has been completed the formal process of writing would begin.

Adding questions to your outline is very useful because not only do they make the book better and more dense because by answering the questions directly the research is improved. Questions can also serve directly as relevant content for your readers.

After the writer has answered all the questions with proper research and the book has been written. The questions listed in the outline can be used to create a new section of the book specifically for listing all the questions and providing their associated answers. This section of your book could come at the end and be called something like "FAQ" or similar. Or you can use the questions as a free giveaway in exchange for a reader's email address to help with marketing.

Regardless of how the questions are used when writing your book, adding as many as you can to your outline will ultimately provide more value to your readers, and make your books better.

Adding Outside Resources to a Book's Outline

The third and final part of a good outline, is the outside resources section. Typically the outside resources of an outline should be consumed by the writer before any research is started and any questions are answered. Outside resources are anything that is not a written book regarding what you are writing about.

Good outside resources to list in your outline would be podcasts, YouTube videos, blog posts, and forum posts all related to the topic of your book. These types of outside resources are easily consumable for a writer and serve as a great way for the writer to get introduced to the topic before beginning proper research.

Given that you spend adequate time creating an outline, and you are as detailed as possible, during this step. When adding these three types of information i.e. a listing of the most important topics found from other books on the same subject, adding as many questions as possible related to the topic, and finally adding outside resources like podcasts and blog posts. Your outline will produce a well-rounded book which does a good job of covering the subject matter well for readers.

After a proper outline has been created for your book. You can move on to the third step in the publishing process: getting your book written.

Methods of Getting Your Book Written and the Best Method to Choose

In regards to getting your book written there are two methods. You can either write the book yourself, which not recommended, or you can outsource the work.

Writing the book yourself is not recommended because your goal when self-publishing is getting things done from start to finish. Outsourcing is best because it gives you the best chance at actually getting your book finished.

Honest Reasons Why You Should NOT Write Your Own Books

The problem with trying to write a book yourself is you are very unlikely to finish the work. Think about writing 40 to 50 pages on a given topic. How realistic is this, if you are not a writer? It is certainly possible and we will briefly discuss the best method for doing it. But it is absolutely the worst way to get started with self-publishing as a business. If you are reading this book as an author or someone who writes a lot then this is a different case. But for the average person looking to make money online. Trying to write yourself will give you the least chance at succeeding.

Even though we do not recommend that you write yourself. We will discuss a style for doing it. The reason we discuss this is, the way you would write the book yourself and use the outline, is the exact way someone you hire should write it. If the writer you hire has significant experience in writing then it is not necessary to instruct them on how to use the outline. But if they have little history you should read this section on how to write yourself and instruct your hired freelancer in the same methods.

A Straightforward Method for Writing a Book and How to Use an Outline

Let's discuss how to write a book yourself and how to properly use the outlines we created earlier, in order to get the best chance at finishing the task of self-publishing a book.

After spending adequate time creating a book's outline and filling the outline with as many details, questions, and resources as possible. Make extensive use of that outline to write the book.

The first thing that should be done when beginning to write a book is to consume the outside resources listed in the outline. Any podcasts listed should be listened to, all forum posts should be read, every YouTube video watched, etc.

Once the outside resources have been consumed the writer should have a good general idea of what they will be writing about.

After the writer has a general idea of the book's subject matter. It is time to begin the formal process of research. As mentioned earlier, when we discussed how questions in an outline should be used, the writer can either begin to perform the main task of researching the bulleted topics then address the outline's questions or vice versa. The writer can research and answer the questions first then begin researching the bulleted topics or the writer researches the bullets then answers the questions.

When the outline was created the main topics should have been placed strategically i.e. the information that was listed first in the outline, is the information that should be written about first in the book. Likewise, the information at the end of the outline should be placed at the end of the book.

Once the writer has performed all their research and begins actually writing. The content should be placed with the same chronological order of the bulleted list throughout the book.

The writer should go topic-by-topic and write, until everything in the bulleted list has been written about. Once everything has been completed the writer should proof read and edit their work. Then submit the work for payment.

Before we address the important topic of how large books should be when self-publishing let's briefly talk about the formal process of research and a method for doing it.

The Simplest Technique for Performing Research

To perform proper research a writer should start from the top of the outline's main topics and begin to research each one. "Research" is finding resources online or in print that explain the given topic in detail. The actions to be performed for each topic is fairly straight forward when publishing non-fiction books. The writer should take the topic and perform online searches. As the writer browses the results from the searches they should look for webpages that are most relevant to providing details and explanations of the thing begin researched.

As resources are found and webpages are read the writer should keep track of the links they are finding. All relevant links should be placed directly in the outline under its associated topic. And when the writer believes they have found enough resources to write about a given topic adequately they should move on to researching the next topic in the bulleted list.

Answering questions in the outline should be performed in this manner as well. The writer should continue performing research in this manner i.e. researching each item in the bulleted list until every topic in the outline has links which explain it.

After all the links have been collected the writer would either begin writing the book or answering the outline's questions.

If the writer chooses to answer the outline's questions after performing their research. They will be able to effectively gauge how good their research was. If answering the questions does not require further research then the writer most likely did a good job researching the main topics. If the writer has a hard time answering questions then more research should be performed.

Once the research has been adequately completed in this manner the writer can begin creating content like we mentioned in the earlier section.

How Large Should a Self-Published Book Be?

When getting started with self-publishing you should have an initial investment. Regardless of the investment amount you have, the goal at this point is to turn your initial investment into as many books as possible.

For each book you successfully self-publish there is an average amount of money you should make each month from that book. The more books you can create in your first 6 months the better. More books will typically yield more income through royalties.

With this goal in mind i.e. publishing as many books as possible with your initial investment. The length of your books in the beginning should be shorter.

As your publishing business grows and you become more comfortable with the process of selling books, and you start to make more money, you should work on increasing the size of the books you are publishing.

Larger books will have increased costs, and require more experienced writers due to the longer length of the work they are creating. So when beginning focus on getting the most from your initial investment.

To determine the size of a book determine the amount of words the book will have. Setting the amount of words also determines how much the book will cost.

You will pay your writers by the number of words they write for you and your rate should be $1.00 for every 100 words written. So a 5000 word book will cost around $50 without fees, 3000 words $30, and so on.

The ideal size of a self-published book is around 100 to 150 pages. Readers enjoy works of this length the most. Of course, if you can publish books which are longer you should, but again remember that publishing books this size will cost more, and require a good writer.

To make a book that is 100 to 150 pages the amount of words should be around 15,000 to 20,000. With this number of words, and a trim size of 5" x 8" typically you will find that once the book is formatted properly it will fall within the ideal page range.

We already know the costs per word for a self-published book. So publishing, a 15,000 word book, will cost $150 dollars without fees. Ultimately publishing multiple books this size, each week, with good quality, should be your goal. But this is not where you want to start because it isn't feasible in the beginning due to increased freelancer costs.

When first getting started you should try to publish books that are 3,000 to 5,000 words. Stick to this range for the first 6 months. Publishing 3,000 word books should get you about 2-3 books for every $120 of initial investment, opposed to 1 larger book.

Over a period of 6 months you want to focus on publishing as many books of this size as possible. After 6 months of staying consistent the income you will be generating at that point should be reinvested back into your business but you want to invest in larger books.

Either begin to publish entirely new books that are larger or focus on making the books you've already published better by adding more content to them. After 6 months of publishing you will have enough experience to make the best decision at that time.

When getting started your books, should not contain pictures, because the only images you should be using in your works are stock photos you pay for. So adding pictures will only increase the overall cost of your books. But in the future, when you begin to publish larger books, you can focus on purchasing and adding applicable pictures to everything which was already published.

Mechanisms for Working Productively

When first getting started. Set specific times per day where you will only work on getting things done in regards to achieving your income goals with self-publishing and force yourself to spend that time working without distractions.

Before you begin working, each day. Make sure you determine in your mind clearly, what it is that you are trying to get done within that time frame. Maybe you want to create 3 outlines, identify 5 book topics, proofread or edit a book, etc. Always know what you want to do before you get started.

If you have multiple tasks to complete within a given time frame, always get started and complete the most important ones first. Do not try to get smaller things done before larger tasks, because these things are not as important.

If you are publishing full-time, then the first thing you should do when starting the day, is to begin working on your most important task. Get that task finished first, then move on to less important things as the day progresses.

This idea of doing your most important tasks first, is an idea from Brian Tracy. Watch his lecture or read his book: *Eat Your Frog*. (If you are interested in learning more about this). This strategy works, because it forces you to work on the most important things each day, and even if you do nothing else, besides that first thing, you will slowly progress toward reaching your overall goal, because you are effectively using your time each day. Your most important task will usually be the task you dislike the most, so this is an easy way to determine it, and this particular thing is what you must complete first daily.

Forcing Focus with the Pomodoro Technique

Another productivity hack which works well for self-publishers is using the Pomodoro Technique. The Pomodoro Technique is a method for forcing productivity as well. Basically you will work for 25 minutes with a timer set, then once the timer goes off you take a break for 5 minutes. Then you continue working for another 25 minutes and take a break for 5. After completing 4 cycles, you take a long break for 30 minutes, then jump back into working in the same manner.

There are apps you can download to help with implementing this strategy or you can use the timer on your phone or a free timer online.

The Pomodoro technique is great for forcing yourself to focus when you find that you are having a hard time doing so. It is not necessary that you use it all the time, but on those days when it seems that you cannot get focused and you keep checking emails, or looking at social media. Use Pomodoro to get working and start being productive.

Within 1 Pomodoro cycle you want to focus on completing 1 task. While the clock is ticking, you cannot look at your email, check your phone, or look at social media. The entire 25 minutes must be directed only for working on the given task. The 5 minute break is allocated for doing those things like checking email or social feeds.

Always start your day focused and knowing exactly what you want to get done. Get started on the most important things first, and leave the small things for later. Try to complete tasks fully, and try to start working, as soon as you get up.

In the case that you are not publishing full-time then set a specific time each day and dedicate that time only for self-publishing. Finally, whenever you work, do it distraction free in an environment where you will not be constantly interrupted.

If you have a hard time getting started, i.e. you can't get focused, use the Pomodoro Technique to force focus. Work consistently for at least 6 months and focus on publishing shorter books in the beginning then work up to larger books as you go.

Follow these rules and you should find that each month the amount of royalties you are receiving will increase.

But you have to remember that consistency and productive focus are the keys, along with patience.

The Role of Enthusiasm in Work and Self-Publishing

One of the hardest parts of starting a business or reaching a goal is finishing tasks once you get started, and staying consistent throughout the entire process. It is very likely that if you tried to write your own book. You would begin with enthusiasm and in this beginning stage you would complete a good amount of work. Then you'll leave your work and come back to it with less enthusiasm.

It's very natural that when you continue to work on the same thing for a long period of time without completion you lose enthusiasm for that thing. And continuing to return to that work will take more and more effort.

Once enthusiasm is lost it is very likely you may give up. Or you may rush to complete the project and decrease the overall quality of the work significantly.

But it should be mentioned rushing to completion is much better than giving up. Although neither situation is ideal when self-publishing or starting any business. Try to stay as enthusiastic as possible with everything you do. Select a niche you are passionate about and hire writers to create your main content. Get your books published completely and these things will help to keep you enthusiastic and motivated to keep going.

OUTSOURCING FOR THE BEST CHANCE AT SUCCESS

The best situation for self-publishing is to use outsourcing to your advantage. The internet has created an environment where everyone is connected. You now have access to 1000s of educated people throughout the world looking for work. By hiring someone and assigning them the task of writing your book you are significantly increasing your chances of getting your work completed properly, within a given deadline, and with a good level of quality. The more you outsource the better the results.

When used effectively, outsourcing, can yield big results, and in a self-publishing business outsourcing will make a huge difference in what you can get done, and how fast you can get it completed.

So use outsourcing, and forget the idea of writing the book yourself, unless you have a good amount of writing talent i.e. you write often like journaling daily, or you have a blog, or you have written plays. Otherwise most people should use outsourcing as their method of getting their books created.

After hiring a writer instruct them to use the outline in the same manner that we discussed earlier. The outside resources should be consumed first, then the main research should be performed, while saving links directly to the outline. The book should then be written when all the research has been completed.

Outsourcing a book as a self-publisher has two parts. Outsourcing the cover and outsourcing the book itself. We have already discussed outsourcing the writing of the book.

This should be done by creating an outline, performing research on the outlined topics, and then having the book written. We will now discuss the 4th step in the self-publishing process which is getting a book cover designed.

THE 2ND ASPECT OF SELF-PUBLISHING A BOOK: THE BOOK COVER

Before we begin to discuss book covers and getting them created properly. It is important to mention that when you hire someone as a writer and assign them their writing task also simultaneously assign the task of creating a book cover. This means that when you hire a writer you should also hire a book cover designer. Even though creating a book cover is listed as step 4 it should be started when you begin step 3.

Always assign writing and book cover design tasks at the same time so you receive all the work necessary to publish the book at the same time. When the writer is finished with her work, the book cover designer should be finished as well. Getting everything back at the same time helps to keep the momentum going when publishing.

Outsourcing the book cover is a simpler task than outsourcing the writing of a book. As your publishing business grows you should work to create a cover design process or workflow. In the beginning when just getting started the goal is to find a designer who is good with Adobe Photoshop.

A Normal Workflow for Designing a Book Cover When First Getting Started

Once a topic for a book has been determined and the book's outline has been created determine an appropriate title for the book and a subtitle. After you have a title and subtitle. And a designer has been hired. Send them your title and subtitle and also send some links to other book covers that you find appealing. Your book cover designer should be instructed to create your cover while using the other covers as inspiration.

A good book cover designer should be able to preserve the overall feel of the inspiration while still creating a cover that is unique. The idea when designing book covers is to create something that looks professional and not self-published. If you hire a designer and only give them a title and subtitle, without any inspiration, the work they will give you back will look self-published.

A better method for getting a book cover designed is to look at other books that are not self-published and use these covers as inspiration for your own self-published work.

Try to find 3 or 4 sources of inspiration for your book cover and send the links to the designer. Let the cover designer work and use their creative process to make a book cover that is different but still similar to the inspiration. You will find that doing this will produce covers that stand out and avoid feeling like a self-published book.

At this point it is understood that you must hire a book cover designer and a writer. But it has not been discussed where to find these people. So let's talk about outsourcing platforms and which platforms are best for certain services.

Platforms for Outsourcing and the Best Uses for Each

There are two places to hire people for outsourcing when just getting started with publishing. These platforms are Upwork and Fiverr.com. Upwork will be your main source of workers and fiverr should serve a secondary source only to be used when first getting started. Fiverr is a great place to initially find a book cover designer at a low cost. And you should use fiverr ONLY for this purpose.

When first getting started look on fiverr for a suitable book cover designer. There are literally 100s of people looking for design work, so finding someone you like should not be too hard.

Go to fiverr and search "book covers". Browse the resulting profiles and look at their portfolios of work. You can look at reviews too but reviews are not important. What's important is a diversity of work, and covers that look professional.

Overall you need someone good with Photoshop, this was mentioned earlier, but it is important to mention again. Prefer people with significant work history but again this not necessary, only a good rule to follow.

When outsourcing your covers you will be sending the designer inspiration so it is not too important that you are totally impressed with their work but you should see that person is creative and has ideally designed different genres of covers and has skills in Photoshop.

You should be paying about $5-10 dollars for a cover and you should also provide the designer with your own stock photos. Create an account on depositphotos and instruct your designer to find their photos from that website.

The designer should use watermarked images for their work initially. Once the final cover is accepted and all revisions have been made to the design and the work is satisfactory, purchase the needed photos from depositphotos yourself.

Cover designers on fiverr like to charge for stock photos, and it is an unnecessary expensive, because you can purchase them yourself.

HIRE A DESIGNER WHO WILL PROVIDE THEIR WORK IN MULTIPLE FORMATS

When you hire your designer talk to them through private message before purchasing a cover. Ask the person if they are okay with providing a .JPG and .PDF for each cover you purchase. The .JPG will be used for publishing digital books and the .PDF is needed to publish print books.

Only hire someone who agrees to these terms for working together. For the cost of one cover they will be providing two formats. Only purchase front covers, do not purchase covers with a front, back, and spine.

For the designer to provide you with multiple formats like you are requesting it is simply a matter of saving their work differently so make sure to hire someone who is okay with this. This simple practice will save you significant money over the long term.

USING STOCK PHOTOGRAPHY AND A WARNING AGAINST USING FREE STUFF

Do not use free photos that you find online and make sure the cover designer is not doing this as well. Using non-professional photos will show so avoid this practice entirely. Never use anything that you find online, in your books. Even in the case of writing. Everything you publish should be unique, meaning any information that a writer finds online must be rewritten.

It is very important that you get in the habit of purchasing your own stock photographs from depositphotos for everything you do with publishing because this is the cheapest option and using stock photos also prevents you from having any possible copyright strikes placed on your account.

Again do not use free pictures from online even though there are methods for finding images which are labeled for reuse and are copyright free.

Always pay for photos because the quality of the photos you pay for will be much higher and provide readers with a much more professional feel.

Simplified Principles for Book Cover Design

Follow these simple rules when hiring your cover designer and you'll produce high quality covers that get attention and sell well:

- Find a designer on fiverr.com when first starting transition to Upwork as you are publishing more books per week consistently.
- Purchase your own stock photos from depositphotos.
- Provide inspiration to your designer based on similar covers you think look good which are not self-published.
- All covers should be assigned at the same time the writing work is assigned.

THE DIFFICULTY OF BUILDING A TEAM

When you are just getting started with self-publishing, building your team will be the biggest and most difficult task to overcome.

In the world of outsourcing there are a lot of people who want to work, but many of these people will not be consistent. Your goal when hiring, especially writers, is to find the people that are serious about making money, who have good written English, and who are consistent.

Once a team has been built and you trust them, building your library of works and increasing your income will be a very straightforward task. Because the more books you publish the more money you will make, given that the quality of the works stays good and improves over time.

Your writer should be found on Upwork.com and you should pay them $1 dollar for every 100 words they write for you. After paying the freelancer fees and also the Upwork fees you will be spending about $1.33 for every 100 words written. Book covers should cost from $5 to $10 each.

How to Find Your Writer and the Specifics of Job Postings

In regards to finding a writer you want to make a job posting on Upwork. Always mention that you are looking for serious people, with good written English, and prefer countries outside the United States to get the most value.

When making a posting on Upwork you can choose to require a cover letter but I would recommend that you do not require it. You can also write some questions for each applicant to answer.

In one of the questions always ask the applicant to provide a sample of their best writing, and you should read this sample closely.

It is also important to include a simple trivial question for everyone to answer. This question is used to immediately eliminate the people who do not have attention to detail and copy and paste answers into their applications without reading.

The Interviewing Process and Hiring

The interviewing process should be kept short and to the point, ask the applicant questions regarding the last project they worked on, if they have some experience, and ask them how long it would take for them to complete a certain assignment.

For example ask a question like how long will it take you to complete a 5000 word book. Look for honest answers that are realistic but also understand that people will tend to under-estimate how much time it will take to complete an assignment.

Hire the person you are drawn to the most, and fund the project. Upwork has an escrow service that will allow you to pay for the project, before it is completed. Using the escrow service is very important as it shows the writer that you are serious and there is money to be made if the project is completed successfully.

Once the project is completed you should check the work for plagiarism using a free or paid plagiarism checking service.

As long as the information has not been plagiarized release the funds to your writer, and begin the process of closely proof reading the work.

The most important thing to remember when outsourcing is you are looking for consistency and good quality. You are not looking for perfection. Also remember that building your team and finding very good writers that are consistent and reliable will take time.

Paying Hourly vs. Using Fixed Price Milestones

The most effective method for using Upwork is always using fixed price milestones when paying freelancers.

There are two ways you can pay freelancers on Upwork. Hourly or with fixed price milestones. The fixed price milestone means you will pay a certain amount of money upfront to the freelancer, when you are ready for them to begin working. You and freelancer would come to a mutual agreement on the price and what tasks should be completed for the payment to be released. This is the best way to outsource.

Always pay a fixed price, never pay hourly. And always be clear with your expectations upfront. This means you should know what you want from the freelancer. Paying hourly can lead to dishonesty, and will almost always be more expensive than using a fixed price milestone to complete the same work.

A Simplified Workflow for Paying a Freelancer

The price you pay someone should be the entire price you are willing to spend to get the work completed properly. For example, if you want to hire someone to write a 5000 word book. Hire the person, and set a fixed price milestone of $60.

Before the money is uploaded to the escrow service, you would make your expectations for payment very clear to the freelancer, and make sure they agree. After coming an agreement use the escrow service and add the money to your account.

Once the freelancer finishes their work and you check that it wasn't plagiarized you would then release the money to the worker.

If the work was good, every week you would pay this person $60 for each book they create for you. And your working relationship would continue in this manner for as long as you are working together.

Before hiring someone on Upwork always get their best email address. All communication that you have with your hired freelancers should be through email, not through the Upwork platform. Make this clear to the people you hire. Upwork should only be used for paying people and finding freelancers.

Email should be used as your main form of communication. Also stress that you expect quick responses when communicating.

Overtime you want to pay your skilled team members through PayPal or Payoneer as opposed to Upwork because the fees will be significantly less and your team members will receive their payments much faster.

Upwork should only be used in the beginning for the first 4 months until you have built a relationship of trust with the person.

If your worker cannot get a PayPal or Payoneer account because of their location then this is the only case in which you should continue using Upwork as the payment platform.

Think of Upwork as a way to find people with skills and a platform for building initial trust, but over the long term you want to communicate and pay your team directly. Once your final team has been built you should not need Upwork except to find new team members.

Managing a Team of Freelancers Effectively and a Simple Technique for Forcing Productivity

When managing outsourced workers make sure you have patience. Most tasks will not be completed exactly by their deadline.

A good method for keeping freelancers on track is to email them daily and ask for updates. Send simple emails once a day or every two days to check in and see what work was completed. These types of emails will keep your team on track.

If the person is working as they should be, then it will be easy for them to respond quickly with some updated files. If they are not on track, then you will most likely get a delayed response.

If you email someone asking for updates and they do not respond, keep emailing them every 6 hours until they respond to your inquires. This will usually force productivity because the freelancer will usually do work after being emailed. After implementing this communication technique over a longer period of time with the same people you will find that your team members will start to email you first, and also respond immediately when emailed.

Use daily or semi-daily emails to check in on your workers and keep them on track after you have assigned work.

Know What You Want and Communicate It Clearly

A 2nd very powerful technique for managing people is using clear guidelines when assigning work. Make sure the responsibilities you assign to your workers are extremely clear. We have already discussed this idea when we spoke about effectively using fixed price milestones. But it's worth mentioning again since we are talking about managing people.

Always know what you expect, and clearly communicate these expectations BEFORE hiring someone. The back and forth communication which will occur between you and a freelancer before you hire them, will keep your relationship positive throughout the entire project.

Understand exactly what you want to get to accomplished and assign that work clearly.

Having clear responsibilities will make a huge difference in managing people and it will increase the likelihood that you receive good work that meets your standards.

It is better to micro-manage and get good work, completed on time, than to not micromanage and get bad work and need to hire a new freelancer and spend more money on trying to complete the same thing.

A Management Style to Avoid When Hiring Freelancers

When outsourcing do not be broad. Do not look for people with expertise so you are less involved in the process. Know exactly what you want. Not knowing what you want, and hiring someone to complete a job under these conditions will usually produce subpar results.

Although this type of hands-off method can work it is less effective especially when getting started. It is better to provide significant direction in the beginning and have very clear guidelines. If you are following the instructions given in this book, i.e. you are making outlines, you are providing inspiration, and you are communicating often. You are increasing the chances that you get good work and you are controlling quality.

Overtime you can decrease the amount of direction you give to your freelancers as you come to trust them more and they become accustomed to your standards and understand what is expected of them for payment.

Becoming an Ideal Client That Freelancers Will Enjoy Working With

Always be fair and honest with your team members and treat them with respect. Especially, when you find good team members. Arguably, most people do not need to hear this statement. But if you read some of the reviews written about clients on Upwork you may think differently.

When a freelancer completes their work, and you check it. Pay them. Do not delay in payment. Paying quickly and on-time is important in the beginning to get your team members motivated. After a few times of paying quickly, you'll find that freelancers will trust you more and try to complete their work within or before deadlines.

Be very straightforward and direct with your expectations in regards to the work being submitted to you and the rules that you expect your freelancer to follow in order to be paid. And when everything is complete follow through and pay them.

A policy of clear expectations with honesty and fairness, and paying quickly, is the best way to be a client that freelancers enjoy working with. And when you work in this manner people will always be willing to do more work for you. You can come to people months later, with new tasks and they will usually be willing to accept what you are offering, because they know you are honest.

PROCEDURES FOR AVOIDING DISHONEST FREELANCERS AND PREVENTING PLAGIARISM

Regardless of how good you are as a client, you will possibly hire some dishonest freelancers, and deal with the consequences of this. Before hiring freelancers you should mention that trust is very important to you as their client and manager.

Things like not plagiarizing should be made very clear upfront to your writers. Make sure your writers understand that nothing in their books can be taken directly from the internet. Everything must be rewritten.

This means there should be no quotes in their books, or pictures from online. Everything must be unique and written by them. This is one of the biggest rules to make clear in the beginning.

Stressing these things upfront i.e. that trust is important, and plagiarism must be avoided, will lessen the chances that the person tries to be dishonest and copy and paste their work.

In my personal experience every time I hired someone who ultimately plagiarized their work, I was not very clear in the beginning about not copy and pasting, so it may have made a difference if it was clear I would be checking for plagiarism closely before paying the freelancer.

Also make it clear to your team members that if they must be late with work, they should be comfortable telling you they need more time. Try to emphasis not waiting until the last minute to email you asking for an extension when the work is due. Or not communicating and waiting for you to ask them about their work first.

Effectively Using the Cloud While Self-Publishing

At this point in the self-process you should be assigning tasks to your writer and book cover designer. Make sure to set clear deadlines when you assign work, and remember to check-in daily or semi-daily to keep everyone on track. Soon you will be getting work back, and it is important to mention that everyone must use the cloud for sharing documents and submitting work.

Use the cloud when building your business. Specifically Google Drive.

All the work that your cover designer completes should be uploaded to Google Drive when it is completed. And all your purchased stock photos should be uploaded Google drive as well. When the writer has finished the final version of their work, it should uploaded to Google then you should be informed that the work is ready for inspection.

Setting Up Google Drive for Maximum Productivity and the Importance of Cloud Collaboration

The best way to use Google Drive is to make individual folders for each freelancer on your team. The filename for each folder should be the freelancer's name. After your folders are created you would right click the folder and share it specifically with that freelancer.

When you assign the task of writing to your freelancer upload the book's outline to the freelancer's specific folder and instruct them to download the outline from the drive.

Of course, the outline could be sent through email and this may be faster. But you want to get yourself and your team members accustomed to using the cloud.

Also opening a folder on the drive when you are looking for something is easier then searching through your email.

All of your collaboration, should be done within the cloud. Meaning you should be communicating privately with Gmail (not Upwork), and uploading and sharing documents with Google Drive.

Every task that is completed as you work with your team should be uploaded to the cloud i.e. uploaded to the drive.

The reason to use the cloud is it's a simple method to backup all your work and search within documents easily. Also as long as you have an internet connection you can access your work, this holds true for your team members as well. If you install the Google Drive App on your phone then you can check and view work on your mobile device, and overall the cloud will make you much more productive and mobile.

Overtime you will find that keeping backups of your work will become time consuming and tedious. One way to lessen this task to use Google drive from the beginning and get your workers accustomed to using the cloud as well.

You may find that freelancers will have a hard time with Google drive in the beginning. In fact, you may find it confusing as well. If you understand how to use it, take the time to teach each person you hire how to use the service effectively. If you do not understand exactly how to use it go on YouTube and watch videos on Google drive.

Use Google Drive. Dropbox Will Waste Your Time

As a cloud storage service Google drive is the best. Do not waste time with dropbox because the upload speeds are much slower regardless of your network connection.

Google drive is the best cloud service and as you get accustomed to using it you will see how useful it is, especially for collaboration.

Putting It All Together: Where You Are In the Self-Publishing Process

At this stage in the publishing process you should have selected a niche to publish in, found a related book topic, and a writer and cover designer should have been hired.

The writer from Upwork and the initial cover designer from fiverr. Your writer should have received an outline detailing the most important topics related to the subject they are writing about and the cover designer should have received a few inspiration covers to create their work.

Once you receive the work back from the freelancers, you should check the writing for plagiarism and make sure there are no errors in the covers. After ensuring both things, pay the freelancers and get them started on the next book you would like to publish.

You can now move on the final stage and last steps of publishing a book which are proofreading, formatting the document, and publishing the book to the different platforms.

Ensuring All Your Book's Content is Unique i.e. Checking for Plagiarism

After your book has been completed. The first thing you must do in is check it for plagiarism. You can use a paid service but the free services are just as good. Search for a website called "theseotools.net" and find their free plagiarism checker. This is a great service.

To check your book you must copy and paste 1000 words at a time into the checker and run a scan. The checker will search each sentence in Google and sees if it finds any exact matches online.

Check your entire document and make sure everything is unique. Once you see the content is unique immediately release pay to your worker. After paying your writer send them the next outline, if it is finished.

Remember to always assign your cover work at the same that you assign the writing so everything is completed at the same time.

If you do not have a completed outline at this point, then instruct your writer to wait. Once you publish the book you are currently working on, you would then make a new outline, and get your writer and cover designer started on the new book.

After checking for plagiarism and paying your writer you can begin proofreading. Always keep in mind the importance of quality control in self-publishing.

Proofreading your books, in the style to be discussed, will significantly improve quality. Always proofread when first getting started with self-publishing, even if you instruct your writer to check their work before sending it.

Effective Proofreading: A 2-Step Process

The process of proofreading is a two-step process. Step 1 in proofreading is checking for grammatical errors. And step 2 is reading the entire document and making improvements as you go.

To check for simple grammatical errors start from the beginning of the book and scan each paragraph looking for highlighted spelling mistakes. As you find mistakes, fix them. Typically you will not find too many. Once you have ensured there are no simple mistakes begin to read the entire document from the beginning to the end and start the process of editing.

As you read the entire book edit the work as well. Making edits is adding words and improving the sentence structures to make the English flow better and read naturally.

If reading longer documents is not something you particularly enjoy then try drinking some coffee as you read or drink some tea. This is will increase your ability to focus. It is very important that you proofread without any interruptions and you focus on understanding the language and trying to understand exactly what your writer was trying to say with what they wrote.

My personal experience is that proofreading will be the most tedious task you must get through when self-publishing. But drinking coffee or tea and using Pomodoro cycles to complete the work will help make the task much easier, in my experience.

Your Main Goal When Editing an Outsourced Book

As you read through the book and find that something does not flow rewrite the sentence to improve it. Your overall goal when proofreading / editing is to ensure that the book flows well and makes sense.

When people read your books they should NOT know it was written by someone whose 2nd language is English.

Simply proofreading everything you publish and making small improvements to the language as you read will ensure the document reads like a native English speaker wrote it.

Any repeated errors in the book like unnatural phrases should be noted. After the book has been completely proofread and edited. Inform your writer of what you found and the things they should improve in their next book.

Always point out errors to your writer, even if the same thing keeps occurring. Overtime your writer will stop making these errors. Also you want to stick with the same people. Because as they write more and more their writing ability will improve naturally.

After your book has been completely proofread and edited, you should upload a copy of the edited version to Google drive. You can either share this version with the writer, or keep it in a private folder for backup, but make sure you backup your work, just in case. Proofreading a document will take hours of significant focus, so you want to use the cloud and keep backups of everything.

At this point you should have a good book, with valuable information on a specific niche topic that is error free and well written. It's now time to move on to the next step: formatting the book to be submitted to different platforms for print and digital publication.

Kindle Direct Publishing vs. Createspace: The Main Self-Publishing Platforms

There are two main platforms to use when self-publishing. These platforms are Kindle Direct Publishing (KDP) and Createspace. Every book you publish should be submitted to both places. When you open your KDP account you should simultaneously open an account on Createspace.

Kindle Direct Publishing (KDP) is a platform for publishing digital eBooks, while Createspace is a platform for publishing print books.

The actual process of publishing is really a process of formatting a word document and uploading the formatted document to both KDP and Createspace.

Therefore, when you format a document and upload it to KDP you are technically publishing a digital eBook and making it available for sale as a download. Uploading the same content to Createspace is effectively publishing a print paperback book, and allowing consumers to buy a printed version of your work on demand.

WHY YOU MUST SUBMIT YOUR CONTENT TO BOTH PLATFORMS

It is extremely important that from the beginning you upload your books to both places. Do not upload your books only to one platform, then later on upload to the other. I made this mistake when first getting started, and realistically my monthly royalties could have been much higher from the beginning. To make the most money with self-publishing, especially when you are publishing nonfiction books, upload to both platforms and make your books available digitally and in print.

When formatting a book for publication you must format the work specifically for Kindle and also for Createspace. You will create two versions of every book you publish. One version will be formatted and uploaded to KDP and another version will be formatted and uploaded to Createspace.

SPECIFICS OF FORMATTING A BOOK FOR DIGITAL PUBLICATION

The first step in formatting your book for KDP is to set the page size. The page size of your word document should be the same as the trim size of your print paperback. The trim size of a printed book is its actual physical dimensions for length and width in inches. You can publish books in all different sizes but to keep things simple, if you are publishing normal non-fiction books set your document size to 5" x 8".

To set this page size look for the page layout settings in your version of Microsoft word and set the size accordingly.

The width of your document should be 5" and the height 8". You can do a simple Google search online or look on YouTube for how to do this if you are confused. But this is a very important step to guarantee that your books look proper when published and printed.

Addressing the Front and Back Matter of Your Books

After you have set the document size correctly you should create what's called the "front and back matter" of the book. The front and back matter are supplementary pages that should be included in every book you publish and they simply provide information about the book, you as the author or publisher, or marketing information.

Supplementary Pages to Include in the Front Matter of Your Books

Create a title page, and list the title of the book, the subtitle, the author name, pen name, or brand, and list your publisher name. The next page should be a legal disclaimer stating that you reserve all rights to the information published and it cannot be copied, posted online, and or resold without your explicit permission. To add this page simply look online for free legal disclaimers and include a copy of one in your book. Make sure you read the copyright fully before adding it. Typically these disclaimers will be about half a page of content.

After the legal disclaimer create a page for the book introduction, which should be a simple 2 to 3 paragraph summary of the book. Then create a page for the table of contents. After the table of contents create a page with some basic contact information like an email address you set up for your pen name or brand name.

If you do not have a domain name yet, and do not know how to create an email address do not add this. Do not put a free email service as this will look unprofessional.

Eventually you should purchase a domain name for your publishing operations. Once you have this you can make an email account to list as contact information in all your books. When that is complete update your books accordingly with this email address.

Adding a page to all your books that asks for feedback and instructs readers to email you when concerns or problems arise will help you to avoid bad reviews.

Bad reviews are sometimes averted because you give readers and outlet to express their feelings directly to you as the author or publisher and writing out that email will typically alleviate much of their frustration. Occasionally people will also send you positive emails and these are great to receive are really motivating.

After the contact page you can include a page called "about the author or publisher" and put a simple 1 or 2 paragraph explanation about either accordingly. Keep it short and to the point. Adding this information will humanize your brand and help readers to connect with you. This is everything that should be in the front matter.

Supplementary Pages to Include in the Back Matter of Every Book You Publish

As for the back matter there should be four pages. One page should ask the reader to leave a positive review of the book, if they found value. The next page should ask the reader to connect with you on social media.

Provide links to a Facebook page for your publishing brand or pen name, also add links to twitter or a blog, if you set those up.

Facebook is the most important and over time just listing these links and continuing to publish your books, and promote them through amazon will result in building a sizable following on Facebook or whatever social media outlet you list.

The next page to create in the back matter of your books is a link to your other books on a similar or related topic.

The best way to link to other works is to create an author page on amazon.

Creating an author page is simple, do a Google search for author central and make one. After making this page, you log in, and search for your books then click a link to add the books to the page. You can do this manually after you publish a new book or you can wait a month or 2 and amazon will add the books automatically. Linking to this author page in the back matter of your books is a great way to get people to follow you on amazon, and also to get more sales.

The final and most important page to include in your back matter is your email marketing magnet. If you want to implement a strategy of email marketing to re-promote your books and get more sales over-time then put a link in the back of books to a website you create. The website should give something away in exchange for an email address.

Subscribe to an email marketing service, and give away something relevant to get readers to opt-in. Another book is a great choice for a giveaway, or an audio version of a book, etc. Something simple but related. Place a link to this sign-up page at the end of your book and as you run free promos you will find that people sign up.

To summarize, the front and back matter of your book will list supplemental information about you as the publisher and the book the person purchased. There are a total of 10 pages that should be included. 6 pages in the front matter and 4 pages in the back matter:

- Front Matter
    - Title page
    - Legal Disclaimer
    - Book Introduction
    - Table of Contents
    - Feedback Request
    - About the Author or Publisher
- Back Matter
    - Review Request
    - Social Media Connect Request
    - Link to Author Central Profile

- Email Marketing Magnet

Make sure your book contains these pages, as adding these pages to the front and back matter of your books will a make a big difference in your engagement with readers.

CONVENTIONAL BOOK FORMATTING PRACTICES

A good practice when getting started is to create a document that is 5"x 8" and add all these pages to it with placeholders for text. Save this document as your book template and re-use copies of it every time you are ready to publish a new book. The first step of your formatting process will be to make a copy of the template and update the text placeholders accordingly.

Once the front and back matter has been created you can begin the process of actually formatting your books. Remember that all your books will be submitted to two platforms and made available for sale in two mediums i.e. digital and print. Digital eBooks are published by submitting your book to KDP and the print version of your book will be made by submitting your content to Createspace.

The first step in formatting is to apply styles to your entire word document for KDP. Make sure the page size is set to 5" x 8" then make sure the font size of the book is set to 14 point Arial. Start the beginning of every chapter on a new page by using the keyboard shortcut CTRL + ENTER.

Avoid repeatedly pressing enter to move content around as this is will not format properly on kindle devices. Always press CTRL + ENTER to move content to a new page when formatting with Microsoft Word.

Conventional Line Spacing Practices and the Application of Section Headers

Do a search online for how to set line spacing in a word document. You can find the line spacing setting under the paragraph settings in most versions of Microsoft Word.

Most conventionally printed novels have increased line spacing, so increase this setting in your books as well.

Increasing the line spacing will make your book more readable in print. 1.15 is a good amount but you can decrease or increase this number based on your preference. After the font size has been set and you have increased the line spacing, make sure all the chapters start on a new page. Once every chapter begins on a new page, the entire document should be set to Arial 14pt font, then you can begin to format the section headings in your book.

Highlight the chapter headings for each section of your book and apply the "Heading 1" style to each.

Every other section heading within the chapter should have the "Heading 2" style applied. Applying styles in this manner will allow you to create a proper clickable table of contents automatically without having to manually add or update page numbers.

Apply your chapter headings and section headings appropriately then make sure all the font colors are black and Arial. Remember that the font size of the main text should be 14pt and the font size of the section and chapter headings should be 16pt.

After these styles are set navigate to your table of contents page and go to the references section of Microsoft word. Click the dropdown under table of contents and click customized table of contents.

For the kindle version of your book you want to remove all the page numbers then add the table. Do a Google search for adding a table of contents with no page numbers in Microsoft word, if this step is confusing. It's a very simple process once you have done it a few times.

Once the table of contents has been added you should see a list of chapters and section headings and everything should be clickable if you press and hold the CTRL key and click a section heading in the table.

Again ensure that your font size is 14pt for the main text of your book. Make sure the headings are correct, your title and subtitle are correct, then inspect the table of contents and make sure it is clickable.

Finally read through your front and back matter and ensure the links are clickable and there are no mistakes.

Now then save the word document as the final version for uploading to KDP. Upload a copy of the document to your Google drive for backup then you can begin the formatting process for Createspace.

Important Aspects Related to Formatting a Book for Print Publication

Make a copy of the kindle document and rename the file to identify the difference between the digital and print versions. Open the print version and highlight all the text. Press CTRL + A to highlight everything then change the font to Times New Roman or Georgia.

These fonts are standard for printed books. After the fonts have been changed you want to add page numbers to the entire document. To add page numbers navigate to section called INSERT in Microsoft Word and insert page numbers where you like. Typically page numbers are put in the bottom right of the book.

After adding the page numbers go to your table of contents and delete it. For this version of the book you want to add a new table of contents that includes the page numbers. Add a table of contents that has page numbers, and make sure the numbers are correct. If you find that the numbers are incorrect. Right click anywhere in the table and select "update table of contents" and the page numbers should change automatically.

Ensure that the numbers are correct then save the document. Also save the document as a .PDF then close everything. If word prompts you to save again after creating the .PDF version, save the document a 2nd time.

Now upload a copy of your word document and .PDF to your Google Drive for backup.

At this point you have completed the most important aspects of conventional book formatting and you now are ready to upload your books and make them available for sale.

The Final Step in Publishing i.e. Submitting Content to the Different Platforms

At this point you are on step 7 in the publishing process. You should have a formatted book in two versions. A Word document and a PDF.

When uploading books to Createspace always submit a .PDF. When uploading to KDP submit the .DOCX or .DOC i.e. the native word formats.

The uploading process is very straightforward. Login into your KDP account and click to submit a new book. Add your title and subtitle information then follow the steps outlined and be as detailed as possible.

The most important thing to remember with uploading to KDP is to set your keywords and categories appropriately. Setting proper categories will improve sales over the long term.

Understanding the Two Parts to a Good Book Blurb or Production Description

Creating book blurbs or product descriptions can be a complicated task depending on how detailed you want the blurb to be, but for the sake of just getting started there are two methods you can use to complete this task quickly.

Before discussing the two methods for creating a book blurb understand that there two parts to every blurb. When we use the phrase "book blurb" we are referring to the Amazon product description for your book. You must enter information into the product description when submitting your books for publishing.

These product descriptions or "book blurbs" should contain two parts:

The first part of a book blurb is a summary of the book in paragraph form.

The 2nd part of a blurb is a bulleted list of the most important things a reader will learn after purchasing and reading the book.

Every book blurb should begin with a catchy headline that should draw attention and make a reader want to review the entire product description.

The bulleted list of important things from the book should have a headline like: "This is what you will learn after reading this book". You would then begin to create bullets and list as many things as possible.

Remember each bullet point should be a sentence explaining some fact or knowledge a reader will gain from reading the entire work. Statements related to facts or statistics which are mentioned in the book work well in this section.

For example, let's say you have a book on interior design and somewhere in the book you mention there are seven primary colors in color theory. You would turn this statement into a sales bullet by writing something like: "You will learn: the exact number of primary colors taught in modern color theory and why this matters for interior designers."

As you write the book blurb continue to create as many of these statements as possible. The longer your bulleted list, the better, and when an interested reader takes the time to read your entire product description a longer list will improve your chances that the person clicks buy.

Creating the bulleted list is the hardest part of creating a product description. The first part i.e. the book summary is fairly straight forward. Just write 1 or 2 paragraphs that summarize the entire book. The longer the summary the better, but at a minimum your summary should be about 1 paragraph and ideally the summary would be 3 paragraphs.

Two Methods for Getting a Book Blurb or Product Description Created Efficiently

To get a book blurb completed there are two methods. You can write the entire thing yourself after your book has been formatted and is ready for publication or you can outsource a part of the blurb writing task your writer.

To outsource the first part of the blurb (the book summary) instruct your writer to create a 3 paragraph summary of the book after he or she finishes writing the book completely.

This summary would be put in the front of the book before the book is submitted for payment. It is very important to stress that the summary be created after the book is written because, waiting to write the summary will make the overall task much easier. It should be easy for your freelancer to write three paragraphs after they have completed all their research and wrote the book.

Once the writer creates these paragraphs you would then take the summary and use it in your book blurb as the first part.

When using this method you will still have to write the 2nd part of the blurb by hand i.e. writing the bullets and creating an attention grabbing headline for the blurb.

Once the blurb has been written you should apply some basic HTML style tags to everything then copy / paste the blurb into the appropriate field when uploading your book to both platforms.

The same description that you use for the KDP version of your book should be used when uploading your content to Createspace.

Save your blurb then go through the process of uploading your book to both KDP and Createspace. The upload process is fairly straightforward, just make sure to think about the categories and keywords you are setting to describe your book.

Your First Book is Officially Published. Now What?

Once the book has been uploaded to both platforms and approved for publishing. Wait a day or two then run a free promo.

Make your book free for 5 days. At this point you have fully self-published your first book and finished all steps.

Congratulations.

After your first book has been published, you can bask in the enjoyment of completing the task of self-publishing a book from start to finish while focusing on quality control.

Now that your book is published the fun part begins. The consistency part. Repeat the entire process again, and publish another book. Then repeat it all again.

As you continue to repeatedly publish books focus on doing it faster, and improving quality.

Continue to point out repeated writing mistakes to your freelancers and help them improve.

When you are proofreading books focus on improving the English more. And make sure you stick to the same niche, and do not jump around.

Stay consistent, stay focused, and be patient, success will come with determination.

STAYING TRUE TO THE SUBTITLE: ENSURING THE SIMPLICITY OF GETTING STARTED

The subtitle title of this book is: *"Simple Steps to Making Money Online for Beginners from Start to Finish"*.

At this point you have read over 150 pages (in print) regarding the entire self-publishing process. The most important steps needed to publish a book have been explained in throughout those pages.

But some readers may argue the content delivery method was not simple enough.

So to make getting started with self-publishing easier, and to make sure I stay truthful to the subtitle of the book. The following section is a straightforward list of 30 steps to getting started.

30 Simple Steps to Getting Started

1. Make sure that you have an active internet connection and a computer with Microsoft word.
    a. If you do not have Microsoft Word you can download and install Open Office for free.
    b. If you do not have an active internet connection, but you have data on your mobile device. Figure out how to tether your phone and connect your computer to the phone for internet when you begin to work.
2. Find a quiet place to work, where you will be distraction free, and if you live with multiple people who are accustomed to disturbing you, make sure everyone understands that your focus cannot be broken when you retreat to this place to work.
3. Determine the exact amount of money you can safely afford to invest in your first set of books, and determine the exact number of books

this investment should produce given that you publish books with a particular word count.
   a. Remember in the beginning you want to maximize your investment by publishing more books that are smaller in word count, as opposed to larger books. 3K-5K words is a good starting point for maximizing your initial investment.
4. Set a specific goal for the number of books you would like to publish each week consistently based on your initial investment, and write down the total number of books you can publish with that investment.
   a. Try to shoot for publishing 2 – 4 books per week.
5. Get your mind ready to work at this publishing project for at least 6 months without giving up, or jumping into something else.
6. Open a bank account for your royalty payments, or use your personal account.
   a. Get your routing and account numbers ready.

7. Open a KDP account with Amazon, and open an account with Createspace.
8. Enter your tax payer information into each account and also your banking details.
9. Create accounts at Upwork, Fiverr, and depositphotos.
10. Open a Gmail account just for work.
11. If you are not self-publishing full-time pick a specific time during each day, for self-publishing work and determine the number of hours you can dedicate each day to your publishing efforts.
12. Begin to list any hobbies you may have, things you are passionate about, things you would like to learn more about, or subject you are an expert in.
13. Pick a topic from the list you created in step 12 and use this subject as your niche.
    a. When making your selection prefer things you are an expert in or something you are passionate about. If you

cannot determine anything then settle for interests.
14. Choose a pen-name or brand name related to your niche and begin to brainstorm topics within the niche. These topics which fall under the niche will become individual books. Determine as many book topics as possible and write them down in a document.
    a. If you choose golfing, for example, as your main niche, then book subjects can be things like:
        i. Stories of great golfers
        ii. A brief history of golfing
        iii. Golfing for beginners or youth or seniors.
        iv. Advanced techniques for golfing
        v. Golfing equipment guide
        vi. Beautiful golf courses throughout the world
        vii. Golfing resource guide
        viii. Etc.
15. Pick a topic for your first book, and a title and subtitle, look for related

books on the same subject, and list the covers you are drawn too.
    a. Try to identify at least 3 covers you like. These covers will be used as inspiration for your cover designer when making your work.
16. Go to Upwork and make a job posting seeking a writer to create a book for you. Make sure to know the exact number of words your book should be.
17. Wait for job applicants on Upwork for a day or so and begin to browse fiverr.com for a cover designer.
18. As you are waiting for applicants on Upwork. Read the section of this book which talks about making an outline. After reading the section. Make an outline for your first book. Once this outline is finished hire a writer from Upwork and a cover designer from fiver.
19. Send the writer your outline and send the inspiration to your cover designer.
    a. Set deadlines for the tasks to be completed and begin to

check in with your team every day to keep everyone on track.
20. As you wait for the work to be completed by your team, begin to create outlines for your next books. Once all the work has been completed, assign new work for the next book or tell your team to wait until you assign new work.
21. Check your book for plagiarism with a free or paid plagiarism checking service online. If the book is not plagiarized then release the pay to the writer.
22. Read the section of this book on proofreading then begin to edit and proofread your first book.
23. Keep track of repeated errors as you read the book, and after everything is finished inform your writer with some constructive feedback.
    a. Remember being positive will make everyone more enthusiastic. But always be honest and patient.
24. Once the book is proofread you should format the book. Read the section on formatting but in general you want to make two copies of the

document. Set the font size to 14pt in each document, and set the page layout size to 5" x 8".
25. Add the appropriate front and back matter to your book then save one version of the document as a .DOCX for KDP and save another as a .PDF for Createspace.
26. The font type in the version for Createspace should be Times New Roman, or Georgia.
27. Upload the book to KDP and Createspace.
    a. Make sure to fill out all the fields when uploading. The most important thing to remember when uploading to KDP is to pick proper keywords and also set relevant categories.
28. Once the book has been uploaded to both platforms and accepted, wait a day or two. Then run a free promo for the book, and use all 5 days.
29. Get your team started on the next book(s) and continue to repeat this process while improving your workflow, taking in feedback from readers, and trying to work faster.

30. Stay patient and consistent. Anything valuable takes time and effort.

JOIN THE FREE VIDEO COURSE:

HOW TO MAKE 1K PER MONTH WITH KINDLE PUBLISHING

THINKSELFPUBLISHING.COM

HOW TO MAKE
1K PER MONTH WITH
KINDLE PUBLISHING

A Clear Plan with Simple
Steps for Beginners

The hardest goal to achieve with self-publishing will be making the first 1K per month.

After reaching this goal increasing your monthly income becomes a simple mechanical process.

Learn the exact steps to reaching 1K by watching our FREE video course: **How to Make 1K Per Month with Kindle Publishing**.

To access the free course click the link below:

http://thinksp.net/1k

ABOUT THE PUBLISHER

This book was published by ThinkSelfPublishing. Be sure to check out the podcast to learn more about Kindle Publishing.

To find the podcast to:

      http://thinksp.net/podcast

WANT MORE DETAILS?

Learn even more about the self-publishing process by enrolling in the ThinkSelfPublishing Blueprint v. 1.0.

The Self-Publishing blueprint is over 9 hrs of video training in 63 videos for publishing in today's marketplace.

Learn more about the course here:

http://thinksp.net/

CAN I ASK A FAVOUR?

If you found this book interesting, or have otherwise found any benefit in it. Then may I ask that you post a review of it on Amazon? Nothing excites me more than new reviews, especially reviews which suggest new topics for writing. I do read all reviews and I always factor feedback into my newer works.

So if you are willing to take ten minutes to write what you sincerely thought about this book then please visit our Amazon page and post your opinions.

Again thank you!

www.ingramcontent.com/pod-product-compliance
Lightning Source LLC
Chambersburg PA
CBHW050216230526
45470CB00001B/413